Little Pinoy Explorers'

FACTS about the PHILIPPINES

Mary Repollo

This book belongs to:

_____

Copyright © 2024 by Mary Repollo.

All rights reserved.

No part of this publication may be reproduced, distributed, or transmitted in any form or by any means, including photocopying, recording, or other electronic or mechanical methods, without the prior written permission of the publisher, except in the case of brief quotations embodied in critical reviews and certain other noncommercial uses permitted by copyright law. For permission requests, write to the publisher, addressed "Attention: Permissions Coordinator," at repollomary17@gmail.com.

Any facts provided in this book has been checked for accuracy from the time of publication.

Written and Illustrated by Mary Repollo

First printing edition 2024.

ISBN: 978-0-6458805-2-6

The Philippines

is an archipelago with 7,641 islands. An archipelago is a group of islands.

It is located in Southeast Asia together with Malaysia, Thailand and Indonesia.

It also has a cool nickname,

"Pearl of the Orient Seas"

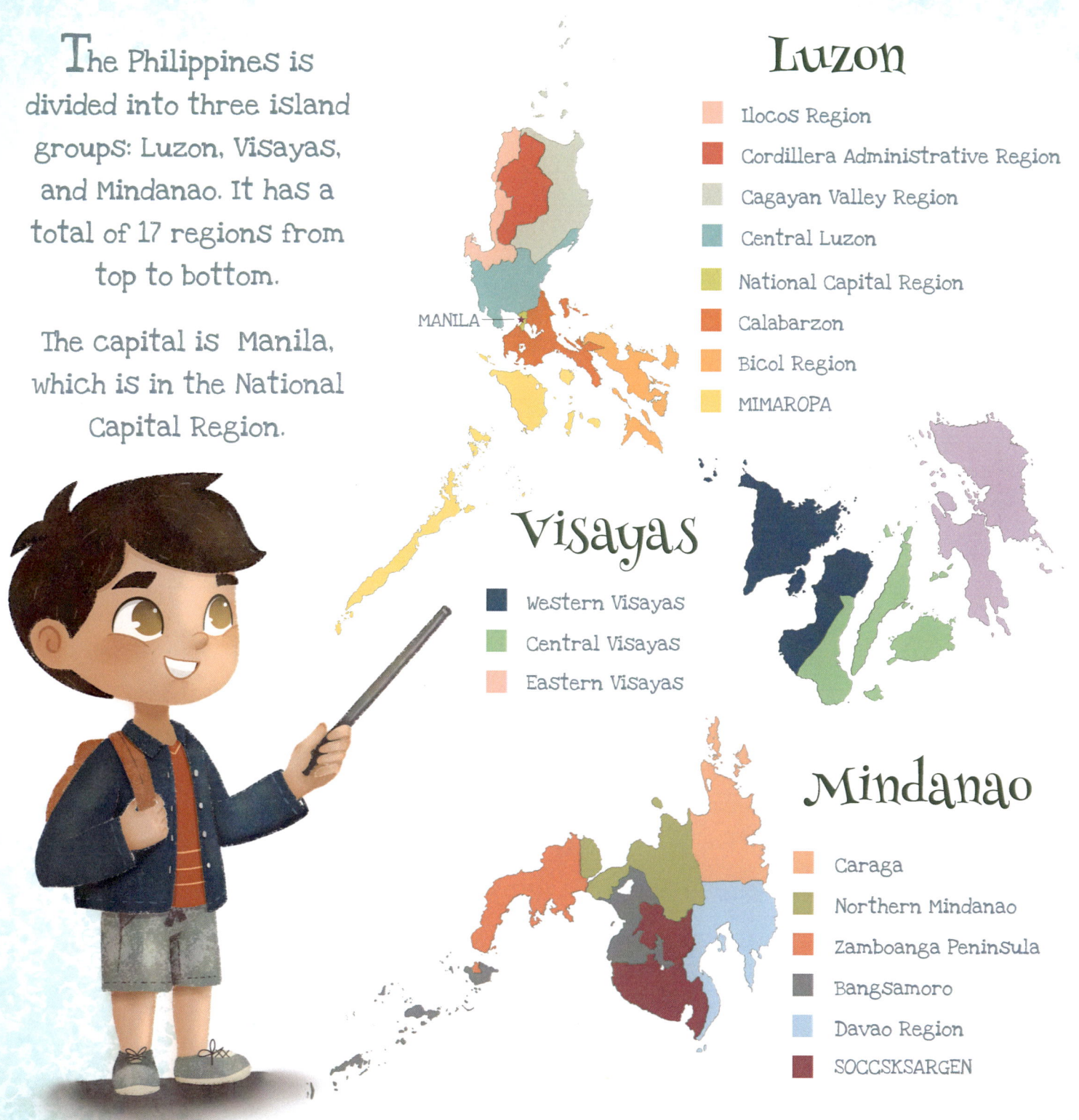

In 1521, **Ferdinand Magellan**, an explorer, landed in Homonhon Island. He named it, Philippines, in honor of King Philip II of Spain.

The official currency is called the **Philippine peso**. However, the first form of coin used before the Spaniards came were called **Piloncitos**.

The coins had a flat base and were inscribed with "MA", which could be the name the Philippines was known to by Chinese traders during that time.

The national anthem of the Philippines is "**Lupang Hinirang**", which means Chosen Land.

When we sing the national anthem we place our right hand over our heart.

Let's sing it together!

Lupang Hinirang

Original

Bayang magiliw,
Perlas ng silanganan,
Alab ng puso,
sa dibdib mo'y buhay.

Lupang Hinirang,
duyan ka ng magiting.
Sa manlulupig, di ka pasisiil.

Sa dagat at bundok,
sa simoy at sa langit mong bughaw,
May dilag ang tula,
at awit sa paglayang minamahal.

Ang kislap ng watawat mo'y,
tagumpay na nagniningning;
Ang bituin at araw niya,
kailan pa ma'y di magdidilim.

Lupa ng araw ng luwalhati't pagsinta,
buhay ay langit sa piling mo,
Aming ligaya nang pag may mang-aapi,
ang mamatay ng dahil sa iyo.

Translation

Land of the morning,
Child of the sun returning,
With fervor burning,
Thee do our souls adore.

Land dear and holy,
Cradle of noble heroes,
Ne'er shall invaders
Trample thy sacred shore.

Ever within thy skies and through thy clouds
And o'er thy hills and sea,
Do we behold the radiance, feel and throb,
Of glorious liberty.

Thy banner, dear to all our hearts,
Its sun and stars alight,
O never shall its shining field
Be dimmed by tyrant's might!

Beautiful land of love, o land of light,
In thine embrace 'tis rapture to lie,
But it is glory ever, when thou art wronged,
For us, thy sons to suffer and die.

This is the Philippines flag.

The three stars symbolize the three island groups, and the rays of the sun represent the eight provinces that revolted against the Spaniards.

 Luzon

 Visayas
 Mindanao

EQUALITY

TRUTH, PEACE & JUSTICE

PATRIOTISM & VALOR

The white triangle stands for equality, the blue represents truth, peace, and justice, and the red embodies patriotism and valor.

Did you know that when the flag is upside down it means the country is at war?

The Philippines is near the equator, which means it is located near the middle of the Earth.

Monsoon...

The rainy season is from June to November,

while the dry season is from December to May.

Summer!!!

The two official languages of the Philippines are:

FILIPINO and ENGLISH

Sen, Agta, Agta-Dumagat, Agusan Manobo, Agutaynen, Akeanon, Alangan, Ata, Ata-Manobo, Ati, Ayangan Ifug obo/Tagabawa, Balangao, Baliwon/Ga'dang, Banao, Bantoanon, Batak, Belwang, Bikol, Binongan, Binukid, Bisaya, Bont kalot/Ilongot, Buhid, Cagayanen, Capizeño, Cebuano, Chavacano, Cuyonon, Davaweño, Dibabawon, Dumagat/Remonta aya, Gaddang, Giangan, Hanunuo, Higaonon, Hiligaynon Ilonggo, Ibaloi, Ibanag, Ibatan, Ilianen Manobo, Ilocano, Iran a, Isinai, Isnag, Itawis, Ivatan, Iwak, Jama Mapun, Kalagan, Kalanguya, Kalibugan, Kamiguin, Kankanaey, Kapampang o, Karay-a, Kirenteken, Mabaka, Maeng, Maguindanao, Majokayong, Mamanwa, Mandaya, Manobo, Manobo-Cotaba saka, Maranao, Masadiit, Masbateno, Matigsalog, Molbog, Muyadan, Obo Manobo, Palawani, Pangasinan/Panggala nan, Ratagnon, Romblomanon, Sama Bangingi, Sama Laut, Sangil, Subanen, Surigaonon, Tadyawan, Tagakaulo, Tagal banua, Tagbanua Calamian, Tau-buid, Tausug, Tboli, Teduray, Tuwali, Waray, Yakan, Yogad, Zambal

Did you know that there are 175 living languages spoken in the country? The top three are Tagalog, Bisaya and Ilonggo

The leader of the Philippines is a **President**, and is voted by the people in an election.

This is a **tricycle**. It is a motorcycle with a passenger cab attached to the side. It can be found in small cities and less populated places.

If you get a chance, take a look at tricycles and jeepneys when you're visiting. Each one is designed uniquely to show off the **Filipino** creativity!

Let's take a quick trip to a few of my favorite wonders of the Philippines!

We're now in the Puerto Princesa Subterranean River in Palawan.

It is one of the world's longest navigable underground rivers. It stretches for about 8.2 kilometers (5.1 miles) and flows directly into the South China Sea.

Did you know that one of the world's largest natural pearls, "Pearl of Puerto," was discovered just off the coast of Palawan? It weighs 34 kilograms (75 pounds) and is valued at around $100 million.

We're now in Batangas, for an exciting adventure!

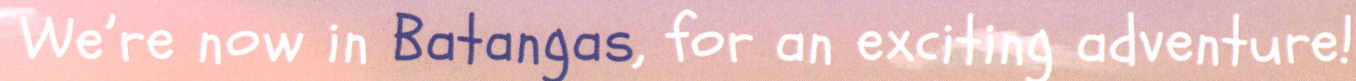

Taal Volcano is considered one of the world's smallest active volcanoes. It can be found within Taal Lake, just like an island. It also has a crater lake in the middle, which is a unique feature.

Did you know that the most recent eruption by this tiny volcano was on March 26, 2022?

Let's stop at Ifugao to see an enormous man-made landmark.

The **Banaue Rice Terraces** is a marvel of human engineering. It was carved by the Ifugao people by hand using basic tools. The local people still plant rice in the "steps" of the terraces to this day.

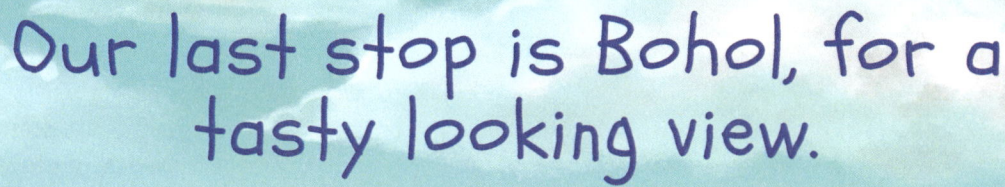

Our last stop is Bohol, for a tasty looking view.

Dry Season

Wet Season

Chocolate Hills are a geological wonder consisting of over 1,200 perfectly cone-shaped hills. During the dry season, the grass-covered hills turn brown, resembling chocolate drops, hence the name.

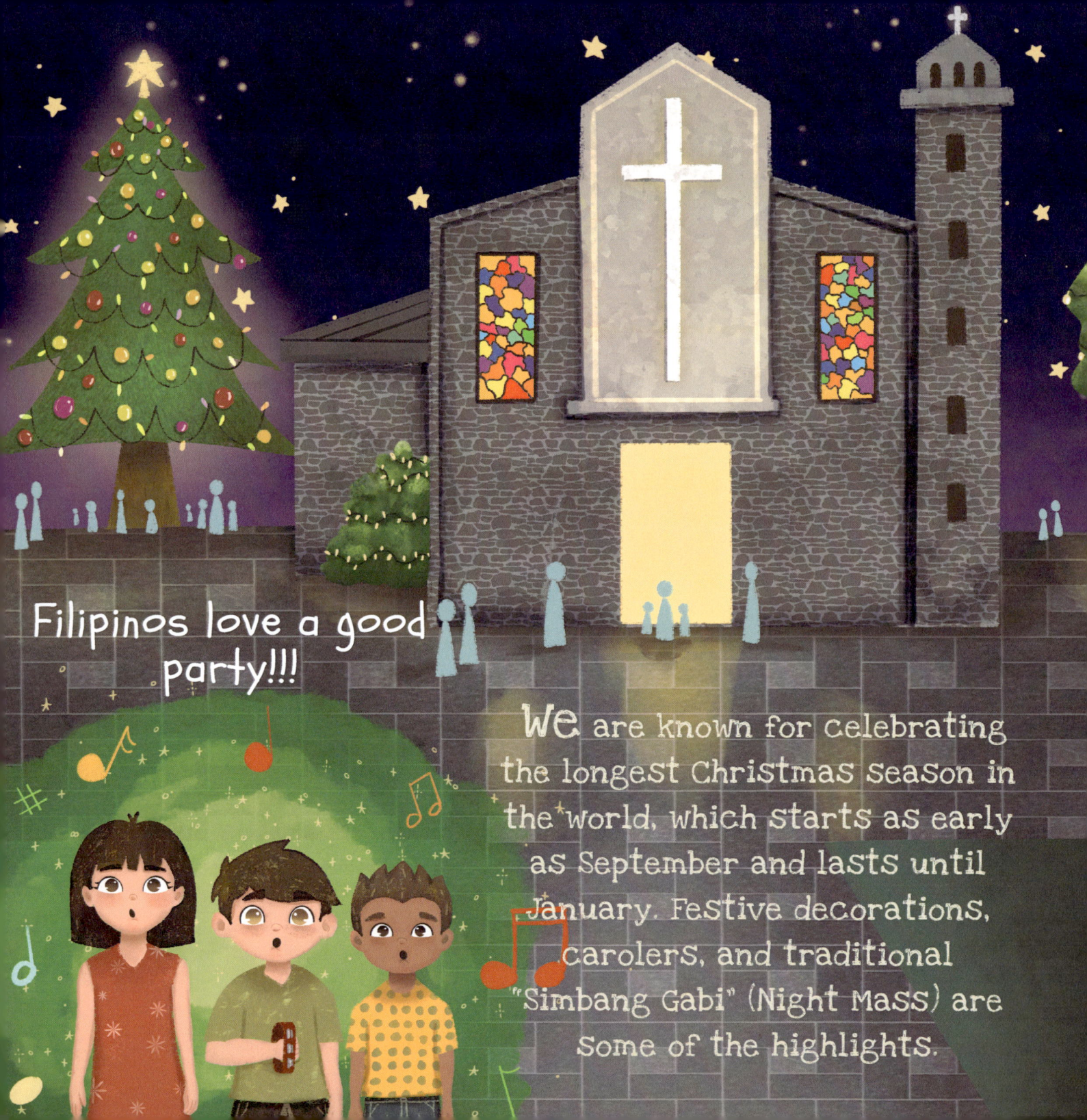

Filipinos love a good party!!!

We are known for celebrating the longest Christmas season in the world, which starts as early as September and lasts until January. Festive decorations, carolers, and traditional "Simbang Gabi" (Night Mass) are some of the highlights.

During the Christmas season, we adorn our homes with "parols," which are intricately designed lanterns made of bamboo and colorful paper. The parol symbolizes the Star of Bethlehem and is a symbol of hope and the Filipino Christmas spirit.

Author's Note

Hi! I'm MARY, a Filipina mom-of-two. I wrote this book for all kids who want to get to know the Philippines, especially migrant kids like mine.

This project of love came from a passing request from my daughter when she expressed her interest in getting to know her cultural roots. It led me down a rabbit hole of internet searches until I decided to create Lil' Pinoy Explorers, with the hope of introducing the Philippines to all children, and build a positive multi-cultural identity as they grow into adulthood.

I hope you enjoy this book together with your kids.

Follow me on Facebook and Instagram at Lil' Pinoy Explorers', for kids content related to the Philippines as well as updates on future book releases and giveaways.

Mary Repollo

www.ingramcontent.com/pod-product-compliance
Lightning Source LLC
Chambersburg PA
CBRC092340290426
44109CB00008B/169